TABLE OF CONTENT

- TABLE OF CONTENT 2
- 1. RIBEYE STEAK WITH BONE MARROW BUTTER 4
- 2. SLOW-COOKED BEEF SHORT RIBS 5
- 3. GROUND BEEF AND EGG BOWL 6
- 4. CLASSIC BEEF LIVER AND ONIONS 6
- 5. BEEF HEART SKILLET 7
- 6. TLET-FRIED BURGER PATTIES 8
- 7. CHUCK ROAST PERFECTION 9
- 8. FILET MIGNON WITH BACON CRUST 10
- 9. BEEF TONGUE TACOS (CARNIVORE SHELLS) 10
- 10. OXTAIL BONE BROTH STEW 11
- 11. CARNIVORE MEATBALLS 12
- 12. BRAISED BRISKET SUPREME 13
- 13. PEPPERCORN-CRUSTED STEAK (OMIT PEPPER FOR ZERO-CARB) 13
- 14. BEEF FAT BOMBS 14
- 15. TRI-TIP ROAST WITH BEEF DRIPPINGS 15
- 16. PORK BELLY CRISPS 15
- 17. BACON-WRAPPED PORK TENDERLOIN 16
- 18. SLOW-ROASTED PORK MUSTER 17
- 19. PORK CHOP DELIGHT 18
- 20. SAUSAGE AND EGG BAKE 19
- 21. CRISPY PORK RIND NACHOS (CARNIVORE VERSION) 20
- 22. HAM HOCK SOUP 20
- 23. CARNIVORE PULLED PORK 21
- 24. PORK LIVER PÂTÉ 22
- 25. LARD-FRIED PORK BITES 22
- 26. CHICHARRÓN CRUST PIZZA (CARNIVORE STYLE) 23
- 27. CRISPY CHICKEN THIGHS WITH SKIN 24
- 28. BUTTER-BASTED CHICKEN BREAST 25
- 29. CHICKEN HEARTS & GIZZARDS STIR-FRY 25

30. CHICKEN SKIN CHIPS 26
31. WHOLE ROASTED CHICKEN WITH DUCK FAT 27
32. CHICKEN WING FEAST 28
33. TURKEY SAUSAGE PATTIES 29
34. DUCK BREAST WITH RENDERED FAT 29
35. GOOSE LEG CONFIT 30
36. GRILLED LAMB CHOPS 31
37. GROUND LAMB BURGERS 32
38. VENISON BACKSTRAP PERFECTION 32
39. BISON RIBEYE WITH TLET GLAZE 33
40. ELK SAUSAGE SKILLET 34
41. HOMEMADE PORK CRACKLINGS 34
42. BEEF JERKY STRIPS 35
43. CARNIVORE DEVILED EGGS 36
44. BONE BROTH SIPPING CUPS OF 36
45. EGG & CHEESE CHIPS 37
46. WILD BOAR ROAST 38
47. LAMB LIVER & KIDNEY SAUTÉ 39
48. CARNIVORE CLOUD EGGS 40
49. SCRAMBLED EGGS WITH BONE MARROW 41
50. BACON & EGG MUFFIN CUPS OF 41
51. SOFT-BOILED EGGS IN BROTH 42
52. EGG YOLK CUSTARD (DAIRY-FREE) 43
53. CREAM CHEESE OMELET ROLLS 44
54. CHEESE-STUFFED MEAT LOGS 45
55. HEAVY CREAM EGGNOG (ZERO CARB) 46
56. BEEF RIBEYE STEAK WITH BONE MARROW BUTTER 46
57. CRISPY CHICKEN THIGHS WITH SKIN-ON PERFECTION 47
58. SAVORY BACON-WRAPPED PORK TENDERLOIN 48
59. LAMB CHOPS WITH ROSEMARY DRIPPINGS 48
60. CARNIVORE BREAKFAST SAUSAGE PATTIES 49
61. GRILLED LIVER AND ONIONS (NON-COMPULSORY) 50

1. RIBEYE STEAK WITH BONE MARROW BUTTER

Prep Time: 15 mins

Cook Time: 15 mins

Total Time: 30 mins

Servings: 2

Ingredients:

For the Steak:

- 2 ribeye steaks (1–1.5 inches thick)
- Salt and freshly ground black pepper
- 1 tbsp olive oil

For the Bone Marrow Butter:

- 2 beef marrow bones, roasted
- 4 tbsp unsalted butter, melted
- 1 garlic clove, chop-up
- 1 tbsp chop-up fresh parsley
- 1 tsp lemon juice
- Salt as needed

Instructions:

1. Preheat the oven to 450°F (230°C) for the roast marrow. For fifteen mins, roast the marrow bones slice-side up up to the marrow is tender. Fill a dish with the marrow.
2. Prepare the butter: Add salt, lemon juice, parsley, garlic, and dilute butter to the marrow. Stir well. Chill up to solid.
3. Prepare the steak by patting it dry and liberally seasoning it with salt and pepper.
4. Sear Steak: In a cast-iron pan, heat the olive oil over high heat. For medium-rare, sear the steak for 3–4 mins on every side. Give it five mins to relax.
5. Serve: Place a dollop of bone marrow butter on top of the cooked steak.

Nutrition (per serving):

Cals: 610, Protein: 42g

Fat: 48g, Carbs: 2g

Fiber: 0g

2. SLOW-COOKED BEEF SHORT RIBS

Prep Time: 20 mins

Cook Time: 3.5 hrs

Total Time: 3 hrs 50 mins

Servings: 4

Ingredients:

- 4 bone-in beef short ribs
- Salt and black pepper
- 2 tbsp olive oil
- 1 onion, diced
- 2 carrots, chop-up
- 2 celery stalks, chop-up
- 4 garlic cloves, chop-up
- 2 tbsp tomato paste
- 1 cup of red wine
- 2 cups of beef broth
- 2 sprigs rosemary
- 2 sprigs thyme

Instructions:

1. Season & Sear: Use salt and pepper to season the ribs. In a Dutch oven, sear in olive oil up to browned.
2. To sauté vegetables, take off the ribs. Add the garlic, celery, carrots, and onion and sauté. Add tomato paste and stir.
3. Deglaze: Scrape off browned pieces and add wine. Slice in half.
4. Slow Cook: Put the ribs back in. Add the herbs and broth. Cook, covered, for 3 hrs at 325°F (160°C) up to tender.
5. Serve: With sauce, skim the fat.

Nutrition (per serving):

Cals: 670

Protein: 45g

Fat: 50g, Carbs: 10g

Fiber: 2g

3. GROUND BEEF AND EGG BOWL

Prep Time: 10 mins

Cook Time: 15 mins

Total Time: 25 mins

Servings: 2

Ingredients:
- 1/2 lb ground beef
- Salt and pepper as needed
- 2 garlic cloves, chop-up
- 2 eggs
- 1 tbsp butter
- Cooked rice or cauliflower rice (1.5 cups of total)
- Non-compulsory toppings: scallions, kimchi, sesame seeds, hot sauce

Instructions:
1. Cook meat: Add garlic to a pan and brown ground meat. Add salt and pepper for seasoning.
2. Cook eggs by frying them in butter up to the yolks are still runny but the whites are set.
3. Put the bowl together: Spoon rice into every bowl, then add the egg and meat on top. Add the toppings of your choice.

Nutrition (per serving):
Cals: 480, Protein: 30g

Fat: 32g, Carbs: 15g

Fiber: 1g

4. CLASSIC BEEF LIVER AND ONIONS

Prep Time: 10 mins

Cook Time: 20 mins

Total Time: 30 mins

Servings: 4

Ingredients:

- 1 lb beef liver, split
- 2 cups of milk (for soaking)
- 2 onions, thinly split
- 2 tbsp butter
- 1 tbsp olive oil
- Salt and pepper as needed
- 1 cup of flour (for dredging, non-compulsory)

Instructions:

1. Soak Liver: To lessen bitterness, soak liver slices in milk for half an hr. Dry by patting.
2. Cook the onions by sautéing them in oil and butter up to they get caramelized. Take out.
3. Cook Liver: If desired, dredge liver with flour. Cook up to browned but still somewhat pink on the inside, 2 to 3 mins every side.
4. Serve: Add sautéed onions on top.

Nutrition (per serving):

Cals: 340, Protein: 28g

Fat: 22g, Carbs: 10g

Iron: 35% DV

5. BEEF HEART SKILLET

Prep Time: 15 mins

Cook Time: 15 mins

Total Time: 30 mins

Servings: 2

Ingredients:

- 1/2 lb beef heart, trimmed and split thin
- Salt and pepper
- 1 tsp smoked paprika
- 2 tbsp olive oil or tlet
- 1/2 onion, split
- 1 bell pepper, split
- 2 cloves garlic, chop-up

Instructions:

1. Season Heart: Use paprika, salt, and pepper to season the heart.
2. Sauté the vegetables: Cook the bell pepper and onion in oil in a pan up to they are tender. Add the garlic.
3. Cook Heart: Cook the split heart for two to three mins on every side over high heat.
4. Serve: This dish tastes best hot, with vegetables on the side.

Nutrition (per serving):

Cals: 320m Protein: 38g

Fat: 18g, Carbs: 6g

Iron: 70% DV

6. TLET-FRIED BURGER PATTIES

Prep Time: 10 mins

Cook Time: 10 mins

Total Time: 20 mins

Servings: 2

Ingredients:

- 1 lb ground beef (80/20)
- Salt, as needed
- 2–3 tbsp beef tlet

Instructions:

1. Form the ground beef into patties after dividing it into four equal parts.

2. Sprinkle salt on both sides of every patty.
3. In a cast-iron pan, heat the beef tlet over medium-high heat up to it shimmers.
4. Fry the patties for 3 to 5 mins on every side, or up to they are cooked to your preferred doneness and have a crust.
5. Before serving, let it rest for a few mins.

Nutrition (Per Serving):

Cals: 420

Protein: 27g

Fat: 35g, Carbs: 0g

7. CHUCK ROAST PERFECTION

Prep Time: 15 mins

Cook Time: 3 hrs

Total Time: 3 hrs 15 mins

Servings: 6

Ingredients:

- 3–4 lb chuck roast
- Salt, as needed
- 2 tbsp beef tlet
- Non-compulsory: garlic powder, pepper

Instructions:

1. Add a substantial amount of salt (and other spices) to the roast.
2. In a Dutch oven, heat the tlet over medium-high heat. Brown the roast by searing it on all sides.
3. Reduce the heat, cover, and cook for 3 hrs, or up to fork-tender, at 300°F in the oven.
4. Give it ten mins to rest before slicing.

Nutrition (Per Serving):

Cals: 520, Protein: 40g

Fat: 40g

Carbs: 0g

8. FILET MIGNON WITH BACON CRUST

Prep Time: 10 mins

Cook Time: 15 mins

Total Time: 25 mins

Servings: 2

Ingredients:

- 2 filet mignon steaks (6 oz every)
- 4 strips bacon
- Salt, as needed
- 1 tbsp beef tlet

Instructions:

1. Secure every filet with toothpicks after wrapping it with bacon.
2. Add salt to the filets.
3. In a skillet, melt the tlet over medium-high heat. Cook steaks for 3–4 mins on every side.
4. Reduce the heat to medium-rare and cook up to the food is done, around 130°F.
5. Take a 5- to 10-min break before serving.

Nutrition (Per Serving):

Cals: 600, Protein: 45g

Fat: 48g

Carbs: 0g

9. BEEF TONGUE TACOS (CARNIVORE SHELLS)

Prep Time: 20 mins

Cook Time: 3 hrs

Total Time: 3 hrs 20 mins

Servings: 4

Ingredients:

- 1 beef tongue (2–3 lbs)
- Salt, as needed
- 1 tbsp beef tlet
- Carnivore Shells:
- 4 eggs
- 1/2 cup of shredded cheese (non-compulsory)

Instructions:

1. Tenderize the beef tongue by boiling it in salted water for two to three hrs.
2. Take out the outer skin and coarsely slice or slice the meat.
3. In a pan, heat the tlet and sear the tongue flesh up to it becomes somewhat crispy.
4. To make shells, fry beaten eggs in a pan with cheese, if using, up to thin tortillas resemble omelets.
5. Serve the tongue flesh within the shells.

Nutrition (Per Serving):

Cals: 510, Protein: 38g

Fat: 40g

Carbs: 1g

10. OXTAIL BONE BROTH STEW

Prep Time: 20 mins

Cook Time: 6–8 hrs (slow simmer)

Total Time: 6 hrs 20 mins

Servings: 6

Ingredients:

- 3 lbs oxtail
- Salt, as needed
- 2 tbsp beef tlet
- Water (enough to cover)
- Non-compulsory: bay leaf, garlic, onion (omit for strict carnivore)

Instructions:

1. Brown the oxtail by searing it in beef tlet.
2. Cover with water and bring to a boil.
3. Cover, simmer, and cook for 6 to 8 hrs, or up to the broth is rich and the meat is tender.
4. Serve meat in soup after skimming fat.

Nutrition (Per Serving):

Cals: 560

Protein: 38g

Fat: 45g, Carbs: 0g

11. CARNIVORE MEATBALLS

Prep Time: 10 mins
Cook Time: 20 mins
Total Time: 30 mins
Servings: 4

Ingredients:

- 1 lb ground beef (80/20)
- 1 egg
- 2 oz finely grated Parmesan (non-compulsory, omit for strict carnivore)
- 1 tsp sea salt
- ½ tsp garlic powder (non-compulsory, omit for strict carnivore)
- 2 tbsp beef tlet or butter (for frying)

Instructions:

1. Combine ground beef, egg, non-compulsory garlic powder, salt, and Parmesan (if using) in a bowl.
2. Make 1.5-inch meatballs out of it.
3. In a skillet, heat the butter or tlet over medium heat.
4. Fry the meatballs for 10 to 12 mins, or up to they are cooked through and browned on both sides.
5. Warm up and serve.

Nutrition (per serving):

Cals: 380, Protein: 30g

Fat: 28g

Carbs: 0g

12. BRAISED BRISKET SUPREME

Prep Time: 15 mins
Cook Time: 3 hrs
Total Time: 3 hrs 15 mins
Servings: 6

Ingredients:

- 3 lbs beef brisket
- 1 tbsp salt
- 1 tbsp beef tlet
- 1 cup of beef bone broth

Instructions:

1. Turn the oven on to 300°F, or 150°C.
2. Add a lot of salt to the brisket.
3. In a Dutch oven, heat the tlet over medium-high heat. Brown the brisket by searing it on all sides.
4. Cover the saucepan closely after adding the bone broth.
5. For three hrs, or up to fork-tender, transfer to the oven and braise.
6. Slice and serve with pan drippings after letting rest for 10 mins.

Nutrition (per serving):

Cals: 520, Protein: 45g

Fat: 38g

Carbs: 0g

13. PEPPERCORN-CRUSTED STEAK (OMIT PEPPER FOR ZERO-CARB)

Prep Time: 5 mins
Cook Time: 10 mins
Total Time: 15 mins
Servings: 2

Ingredients:

- 2 ribeye steaks (8 oz every)
- 1 tbsp coarse salt
- 1 tbsp cracked black pepper (omit for strict zero-carb)
- 1 tbsp beef tlet or butter

Instructions:

1. Dry the steaks with a pat. Sprinkle salt (and pepper, if using) on both sides.
2. In a cast-iron pan, cook the tlet over high heat.
3. Steaks Must be seared for 4 to 5 mins on every side (medium-rare), or up to done to your liking.
4. Give it five mins to rest before serving.

Nutrition (per serving):

Cals: 560, Protein: 48g

Fat: 42g

Carbs: 0g

14. BEEF FAT BOMBS

Prep Time: 10 mins
Cook Time: 10 mins
Total Time: 20 mins
Servings: 6

Ingredients:

- ½ cup of rendered beef tlet
- ½ cup of cooked ground beef
- 1 tbsp collagen powder (non-compulsory)
- ½ tsp salt

Instructions:

1. Over low heat, melt the tlet.
2. Add salt, ground beef, and collagen if using.
3. Pour onto a lined tray or silicone molds.
4. Freeze for 30 to 60 mins to solidify.
5. Keep in the refrigerator or freezer and eat as required.

Nutrition (per fat bomb):

Cals: 130, Protein: 4g

Fat: 12g, Carbs: 0g

15. TRI-TIP ROAST WITH BEEF DRIPPINGS

Prep Time: 10 mins
Cook Time: 45 mins
Total Time: 55 mins
Servings: 6

Ingredients:

- 2½ lbs tri-tip roast
- 1 tbsp coarse salt
- 1 tbsp beef tlet

Instructions:

1. Turn the oven on to 400°F, or 200°C.
2. Sprinkle salt on the tri-tip.
3. In a skillet, heat the tlet. Tri-tip Must be seared for 8 to 10 mins total, on both sides, up to browned.
4. Once inside temperature reveryes 130°F (medium-rare), transfer to oven and cook for 30 to 35 mins.
5. Take ten mins to relax. Serve with the pan's meat drippings on the side.

Nutrition (per serving):

Cals: 460, Protein: 44g

Fat: 30g

Carbs: 0g

16. PORK BELLY CRISPS

Prep Time: 10 mins

Cook Time: 1 hr 30 mins

Total Time: 1 hr 40 mins

Servings: 4

Ingredients:

- 1 lb pork belly, skin on
- 1 tsp salt
- ½ tsp black pepper
- 1 tsp garlic powder
- 1 tsp paprika

Instructions:

1. Turn the oven on to 400°F, or 200°C.
2. Using paper towels, pat the pork belly dry. Make a score on the skin.
3. Add paprika, garlic powder, salt, and pepper to all sides.
4. Place skin side up on a rack set over a baking sheet.
5. If necessary, flip halfway during the 1.5-hr roasting time.
6. After 10 mins of resting, slice into strips or little crisps.

Nutrition (per serving):

Cals: 360, Protein: 16g

Fat: 32g

Carbs: 1g

17. BACON-WRAPPED PORK TENDERLOIN

Prep Time: 15 mins

Cook Time: 40 mins

Total Time: 55 mins

Servings: 4

Ingredients:

- 1 pork tenderloin (1–1.5 lbs)
- 8–10 slices bacon
- 2 tbsp Dijon mustard
- 1 tbsp brown sugar
- 1 tsp garlic powder
- Salt & pepper as needed

Instructions:

1. Turn the oven on to 375°F, or 190°C.
2. Combine Dijon, brown sugar, salt, pepper, and garlic powder.
3. Cover the pork tenderloin with the Mixture.
4. Using toothpicks, attach the bacon strips around the tenderloin.
5. The internal temperature Must revery 145°F after 35 to 40 mins of roasting in a baking dish.
6. To crisp the bacon, broil it for two to three mins.
7. Before slicing, let it rest for five mins.

Nutrition (per serving):

Cals: 410, Protein: 38g

Fat: 28g, Carbs: 3g

18. SLOW-ROASTED PORK MUSTER

Prep Time: 15 mins

Cook Time: 6 hrs

Total Time: 6 hrs 15 mins

Servings: 6–8

Ingredients:

- 4–5 lb pork Muster
- 1 tbsp kosher salt
- 1 tsp pepper
- 1 tbsp paprika
- 1 tbsp brown sugar
- 1 tbsp garlic powder
- 1 tsp cumin
- 1 cup of chicken broth

Instructions:

1. Turn the oven on to 300°F, or 150°C.
2. Rub the pork heavily with a Mixture of all the spices.
3. Put the meat and broth in a roasting pan. Wrap with foil.
4. The meat Must be tender and shred readily after 5 to 6 hrs of roasting.

5. To crisp, take off the foil and roast uncovered for the final half hr.
6. Take a fifteen-min break before shredding.

Nutrition (per serving):

Cals: 450

Protein: 35g

Fat: 33g, Carbs: 2g

19. PORK CHOP DELIGHT

Prep Time: 10 mins

Cook Time: 25 mins

Total Time: 35 mins

Servings: 4

Ingredients:

- 4 bone-in pork chops
- 1 tbsp olive oil
- 1 onion, split
- 1 cup of mushrooms, split
- 1 tsp thyme
- 1 tsp garlic powder
- ½ cup of chicken broth
- ¼ cup of cream (non-compulsory)

Instructions:

1. Add salt, pepper, and garlic powder to the pork chops.
2. Heat a pan of oil and sear the pork chops for 3 to 4 mins on every side. Take out and put aside.
3. Cook the mushrooms and onions in the skillet for five mins.
4. Bring the broth and thyme to a boil.
5. Put the pork chops back in the skillet, cover, and cook for ten mins.
6. For a deeper sauce, you may non-compulsoryly stir in cream.

Nutrition (per serving):

Cals: 390, Protein: 34g

Fat: 25g

Carbs: 6g

20. SAUSAGE AND EGG BAKE

Prep Time: 15 mins

Cook Time: 35 mins

Total Time: 50 mins

Servings: 6

Ingredients:

- 1 lb breakfast sausage
- 8 eggs
- ½ cup of milk
- 1 cup of shredded cheddar cheese
- ½ onion, diced
- 1 bell pepper, diced
- Salt & pepper as needed

Instructions:

1. Turn the oven on to 375°F, or 190°C.
2. In a pan, brown the sausage, then add the onions and peppers and simmer up to they are tender.
3. Whisk together the eggs, milk, salt, and pepper in a bowl.
4. Spread the sausage Mixture in a baking dish that has been oiled, then cover it with eggs.
5. Add some shredded cheese on top.
6. Bake up to the middle is firm, 30 to 35 mins.
7. Before slicing, let it cool somewhat.

Nutrition (per serving):

Cals: 320, Protein: 20g

Fat: 25g, Carbs: 3g

21. CRISPY PORK RIND NACHOS (CARNIVORE VERSION)

Prep Time: 10 mins
Cook Time: 10 mins
Total Time: 20 mins
Servings: 2

Ingredients:

- 4 oz pork rinds
- 1 cup of shredded cheddar cheese (or other carnivore-friendly cheese)
- 1/2 lb ground beef
- 1/2 tsp sea salt
- 1/4 tsp black pepper (non-compulsory)
- 1/4 cup of sour cream (non-compulsory, for serving)
- 2 tbsp cut up bacon (non-compulsory)

Instructions:

1. Turn the oven on to 375°F, or 190°C.
2. Add salt and non-compulsory pepper to a pan and sauté the ground beef up to it is well browned. If necessary, drain.
3. Lay out the pork rinds on a baking table.
4. Add shredded cheese and cooked ground meat on top.
5. Bake up to the cheese is completely dilute, 5 to 7 mins.
6. Serve with sour cream and, if desired, top with cut up bacon.

Nutrition (per serving):

Cals: 480, Protein: 35g

Fat: 38g

Carbs: <1g

22. HAM HOCK SOUP

Prep Time: 10 mins
Cook Time: 3 hrs
Total Time: 3 hrs 10 mins
Servings: 4

Ingredients:

- 2 smoked ham hocks
- 8 cups of water or bone broth
- Salt as needed
- Non-compulsory: bay leaf, herbs (omit for strict carnivore)

Instructions:

1. In a big saucepan, combine water and ham hocks.
2. After bringing to a boil, lower the heat and simmer for two and a half to three hrs.
3. Shred the meat and take out the ham hocks.
4. Put the meat back in the saucepan and throw away the bones.
5. For a further fifteen mins, simmer. Season with salt.

Nutrition (per serving):

Cals: 290, Protein: 28g

Fat: 20g

Carbs: 0g

23. CARNIVORE PULLED PORK

Prep Time: 10 mins
Cook Time: 6–8 hrs (slow cooker)
Total Time: 8 hrs 10 mins
Servings: 6

Ingredients:

- 3–4 lb pork Muster
- 1 tbsp sea salt
- 1 tsp smoked paprika (non-compulsory)
- 1/2 tsp garlic powder (non-compulsory)

Instructions:

1. Apply salt (and non-compulsory spices) to the pork Muster.
2. Put in the slow cooker and cook for 8 hrs on low or 6 hrs on high.
3. Use forks to shred the pork, then serve it either plain or with the drippings.

Nutrition (per serving):

Cals: 420, Protein: 33g

Fat: 32g

Carbs: 0g

24. PORK LIVER PÂTÉ

Prep Time: 10 mins
Cook Time: 20 mins
Total Time: 30 mins
Servings: 6

Ingredients:

- 1 lb pork liver, chop-up
- 1/2 cup of lard or butter
- 1/2 tsp sea salt
- 1/4 tsp ground pepper (non-compulsory)
- 1/4 cup of heavy cream (non-compulsory for texture)

Instructions:

1. Heat 2 tbsp of lard or butter in a pan over medium heat.
2. Cook the liver for 7 to 10 mins, or up to it is no longer pink.
3. Add the remaining lard, cream, and salt to the liver and blend up to smooth.
4. Before serving, let it cool in the refrigerator for at least an hr.

Nutrition (per serving):

Cals: 220, Protein: 18g

Fat: 16g

Carbs: 1g

25. LARD-FRIED PORK BITES

Prep Time: 10 mins
Cook Time: 15 mins
Total Time: 25 mins
Servings: 3

Ingredients:

- 1 lb pork Muster or pork belly, cubed
- 1/2 cup of lard
- Sea salt as needed

Instructions:

1. In a skillet, heat the lard over medium-high heat.
2. Add the pork cubes and cook up to crispy, rotating regularly, for 10 to 15 mins.
3. Drain on paper towels after removing with a slotted spoon.
4. Before serving, sprinkle with sea salt.

Nutrition (per serving):

Cals: 450, Protein: 30g

Fat: 36g

Carbs: 0g

26. CHICHARRÓN CRUST PIZZA (CARNIVORE STYLE)

Prep Time: 10 mins

Cook Time: 15 mins

Total Time: 25 mins

Servings: 2

Ingredients:

- 2 cups of crushed chicharrón (pork rinds)
- 1 cup of shredded mozzarella cheese
- 1 egg
- ½ tsp garlic powder (non-compulsory)
- ½ tsp onion powder (non-compulsory)
- ½ cup of marinara sauce (sugar-free)
- ½ cup of cooked ground beef or sausage
- ½ cup of shredded mozzarella (for topping)
- Pepperoni slices (non-compulsory)

Instructions:

1. Turn the oven on to 400°F, or 200°C.

2. In a bowl, combine cut up chicharrón, shredded cheese, egg, onion powder, and garlic powder.
3. Press Mixture in a circle (like a pizza crust) onto a baking sheet coated with paper.
4. Bake up to golden, about 10 mins.
5. Take out of the oven and add the pepperoni, cheese, meat, and sauce on top.
6. Bake for a further five mins, or up to the cheese is bubbling and dilute.
7. Before slicing, let cool somewhat.

Nutrition (per serving, approx.):

Cals: 480, Protein: 38g

Fat: 35g

Carbs: 3g

27. CRISPY CHICKEN THIGHS WITH SKIN

Prep Time: 5 mins

Cook Time: 25 mins

Total Time: 30 mins

Servings: 4

Ingredients:

- 4 bone-in, skin-on chicken thighs
- Salt and pepper
- 1 tbsp animal fat or butter

Instructions:

1. Add salt and pepper to the chicken thighs after patting them dry.
2. In a pan, heat the lard over medium-high heat.
3. Thighs Must be cooked with the skin side down for 12 to 15 mins without stirring, or up to the skin is quite crispy.
4. Cook for ten more mins after flipping, or up to the internal temperature reveryes 165°F (74°C).
5. Before serving, let it rest for a few mins.

Nutrition (per serving, approx.):

Cals: 320, Protein: 28g

Fat: 23g

Carbs: 0g

28. BUTTER-BASTED CHICKEN BREAST

Prep Time: 5 mins

Cook Time: 15 mins

Total Time: 20 mins

Servings: 2

Ingredients:

- 2 boneless, skinless chicken breasts
- Salt and pepper
- 2 tbsp butter
- 1 garlic clove (non-compulsory)
- 1 sprig rosemary or thyme (non-compulsory)

Instructions:

1. Use salt and pepper to season the chicken.
2. Melt the butter in a pan over medium heat.
3. Cook the chicken for 6–7 mins on every side.
4. Add the herbs and garlic in the last two mins, then baste the chicken with hot butter.
5. When the internal temperature reveryes 165°F (74°C), take out. Take five mins to relax.

Nutrition (per serving, approx.):

Cals: 290, Protein: 35g

Fat: 16g

Carbs: 0g

29. CHICKEN HEARTS & GIZZARDS STIR-FRY

Prep Time: 10 mins

Cook Time: 15 mins

Total Time: 25 mins

Servings: 2

Ingredients:

- 1 cup of chicken hearts
- 1 cup of chicken gizzards (pre-boiled or pressure cooked for tenderness)
- Salt and pepper
- 2 tbsp animal fat or butter

Instructions:

1. In a pan, heat the lard over medium-high heat.
2. Add gizzards and cook up to browned, about 5 mins.
3. Cook for a further five to seven mins after adding the chicken hearts.
4. Serve hot, seasoned as needed.

Nutrition (per serving, approx.):

Cals: 300, Protein: 28g

Fat: 20g, Carbs: 1g

30. CHICKEN SKIN CHIPS

Prep Time: 5 mins

Cook Time: 20 mins

Total Time: 25 mins

Servings: 4

Ingredients:

- Skin from 4 chicken thighs or breasts
- Salt
- Non-compulsory: paprika, garlic powder

Instructions:

1. Turn the oven on to 375°F, or 190°C.
2. Place the skins flat on a baking sheet covered with paper.
3. If using, add a mini pinch of salt and spices.
4. To keep skins flat, place a second pan on top of a second layer of parchment.

5. Bake for 20 to 25 mins, or up to crispy and golden.
6. To serve, drain on paper towels.

Nutrition (per serving, approx.):

Cals: 200, Protein: 10g

Fat: 18g

Carbs: 0g

31. WHOLE ROASTED CHICKEN WITH DUCK FAT

Prep Time: 15 mins
Cook Time: 1 hr 30 mins
Total Time: 1 hr 45 mins
Servings: 4

Ingredients:

- 1 whole chicken (about 4 lbs)
- 3 tbsp duck fat (melted)
- 4 cloves garlic, chop-up
- 1 tbsp fresh rosemary, chop-up
- 1 tbsp fresh thyme, chop-up
- 1 tsp salt
- ½ tsp black pepper
- 1 lemon, halved
- 1 onion, quartered

Instructions:

1. Set the oven temperature to 425°F (220°C).
2. Dry the chicken with a pat. If at all possible, rub duck fat under the skin of the bird.
3. Add thyme, garlic, rosemary, salt, and pepper for seasoning.
4. Place the onion and lemon halves within the cavity.
5. Use kitchen twine to secure the legs together.
6. Put the chicken, breast side up, in a roasting pan.
7. The interior temperature Must revery 165°F (74°C) after 1 and a half hrs of roasting.
8. Before sliceting, let it rest for ten mins.

Nutrition (per serving):

Cals: 540, Fat: 37g

Saturated Fat: 11g

Carbs: 2g

Protein: 45g

32. CHICKEN WING FEAST

Prep Time: 10 mins
Cook Time: 40 mins
Total Time: 50 mins
Servings: 6

Ingredients:

- 3 lbs chicken wings
- 2 tbsp vegetable oil
- 1 tbsp garlic powder
- 1 tbsp onion powder
- 1 tsp paprika
- 1 tsp salt
- ½ tsp black pepper
- 1 cup of barbecue sauce (non-compulsory, for coating)

Instructions:

1. Turn the oven on to 400°F, or 200°C.
2. Combine the wings, oil, and spices in a Big basin.
3. Arrange in a single layer on a baking sheet.
4. Bake up to golden and crispy, flipping once, 35 to 40 mins.
5. If desired, toss with barbecue sauce before serving.

Nutrition (per serving):

Cals: 380, Fat: 28g

Saturated Fat: 8g

Carbs: 3g

Protein: 29g

33. TURKEY SAUSAGE PATTIES

Prep Time: 10 mins
Cook Time: 10 mins
Total Time: 20 mins
Servings: 4 (8 patties)

Ingredients:

- 1 lb ground turkey
- 1 tsp fennel seeds
- 1 tsp sage
- ½ tsp garlic powder
- ½ tsp onion powder
- ¼ tsp crushed red pepper flakes
- 1 tsp salt
- ½ tsp black pepper
- 1 tbsp olive oil

Instructions:

1. In a bowl, thoroughly combine all ingredients (omit oil).
2. Make eight little patties.
3. In a skillet, heat the oil over medium heat.
4. Cook patties at 165°F/74°C for 4 to 5 mins on every side, or up to browned and cooked through.
5. Warm up and serve.

Nutrition (per serving):

Cals: 230, Fat: 13g

Saturated Fat: 3g

Carbs: 1g

Protein: 27g

34. DUCK BREAST WITH RENDERED FAT

Prep Time: 10 mins
Cook Time: 15 mins

Total Time: 25 mins
Servings: 2

Ingredients:

- 2 duck breasts (skin-on)
- Salt and pepper as needed

Instructions:

1. Make crosshatch marks on the duck breasts' skin.
2. Add salt and pepper for seasoning.
3. Transfer to a cool skillet, skin-side down.
4. Cook over medium heat for 7 to 8 mins, or up to the skin is crispy and the fat has been rendered.
5. Cook for a further 4 to 5 mins after flipping, or up to done.
6. Before slicing, rest for five mins.
7. For use in other recipes, save aside rendered duck fat.

Nutrition (per serving):

Cals: 460, Fat: 35g

Saturated Fat: 11g

Carbs: 0g

Protein: 36g

35. GOOSE LEG CONFIT

Prep Time: 20 mins
Cook Time: 2 hrs 30 mins
Total Time: 2 hrs 50 mins
Servings: 2

Ingredients:

- 2 goose legs
- 1 tbsp salt
- 1 tsp black pepper
- 4 cloves garlic, smashed
- 2 sprigs thyme
- 2 cups of rendered goose fat or duck fat

Instructions:

1. Use thyme, garlic, salt, and pepper to season goose legs.
2. Refrigerate overnight with a lid on.
3. Rinse and wipe dry to take out excess salt.
4. Put the legs in a deep pan and pour duck or goose grease over them.
5. Simmer for 2.5 hrs on low heat (250°F/120°C) up to tender.
6. Let to cool in fat. Before serving, reheat by crisping the skin in a hot pan or oven.

Nutrition (per serving):

Cals: 700, Fat: 58g

Saturated Fat: 18g

Carbs: 1g

Protein: 45g

36. GRILLED LAMB CHOPS

Prep Time: 15 mins
Cook Time: 10 mins
Total Time: 25 mins
Servings: 4

Ingredients:

- 8 lamb loin chops (about 1-inch thick)
- 3 tbsp olive oil
- 4 cloves garlic, chop-up
- 2 tbsp fresh rosemary, chop-up
- 1 tbsp fresh thyme, chop-up
- 1 tsp salt
- 1/2 tsp black pepper
- 1 lemon, juiced

Instructions:

1. In a bowl, combine together lemon juice, olive oil, garlic, rosemary, thyme, salt, and pepper.
2. For a richer flavor, rub the lamb chops with the Mixture and let them marinade for 30 mins.
3. Set the grill's temperature to medium-high.

4. For medium-rare, grill lamb chops for 4 to 5 mins on every side.
5. Before serving, let it sit for five mins.

Nutrition (per serving):

Cals: 340 | Protein: 28g | Fat: 25g | Carbs: 1g | Fiber: 0g

37. GROUND LAMB BURGERS

Prep Time: 10 mins
Cook Time: 10 mins
Total Time: 20 mins
Servings: 4

Ingredients:

- 1 lb ground lamb
- 1 garlic clove, chop-up
- 1 tsp ground cumin
- 1 tsp smoked paprika
- Salt and pepper as needed
- 4 burger buns
- Toppings: red onion, lettuce, tomato, tzatziki (non-compulsory)

Instructions:

1. Combine the ground lamb, paprika, cumin, garlic, salt, and pepper in a bowl.
2. Make four patties.
3. Grill or pan-fry for 4 to 5 mins on every side over medium-high heat.
4. Top with your preferred toppings and serve on buns.

Nutrition (per serving without bun/toppings):

Cals: 280 | Protein: 22g | Fat: 22g | Carbs: 0g

38. VENISON BACKSTRAP PERFECTION

Prep Time: 10 mins
Cook Time: 8 mins
Total Time: 18 mins
Servings: 2

Ingredients:

- 1 lb venison backstrap (whole or medallions)
- 2 tbsp butter
- 2 cloves garlic, crushed
- 1 sprig rosemary
- Salt and pepper as needed

Instructions:

1. Use salt and pepper to season the venison.
2. Melt butter in a cast-iron pan over high heat and add the garlic and rosemary.
3. For medium-rare, sear the backstrap for 3–4 mins on every side.
4. While cooking, baste with garlic butter.
5. Before slicing, let it rest for five mins.

Nutrition (per serving):

Cals: 260 | Protein: 35g | Fat: 13g | Carbs: 0g

39. BISON RIBEYE WITH TLET GLAZE

Prep Time: 10 mins
Cook Time: 10 mins
Total Time: 20 mins
Servings: 2

Ingredients:

- 2 bison ribeye steaks (8 oz every)
- 2 tbsp beef tlet
- Salt and pepper
- Fresh herbs (thyme, rosemary)

Instructions:

1. Let steaks come to room temperature. Add salt and pepper for seasoning.
2. Turn the heat up to high in a skillet or grill.
3. For medium-rare, sear steaks for 3–4 mins on every side.
4. Add the herbs and tlet at the last min and ladle them over the meat.
5. Give it a 5-min rest before serving.

Nutrition (per serving):

Cals: 400 | Protein: 38g | Fat: 28g | Carbs: 0g

40. ELK SAUSAGE SKILLET

Prep Time: 10 mins
Cook Time: 20 mins
Total Time: 30 mins
Servings: 4

Ingredients:

- 1 lb elk sausage, split
- 1 bell pepper, split
- 1 onion, split
- 1 zucchini, chop-up
- 2 tbsp olive oil
- 1 tsp Italian seasoning
- Salt and pepper as needed

Instructions:

1. In a Big pan, heat the olive oil over medium-high heat.
2. After five mins, add the sausage pieces and brown them.
3. Cook the zucchini, peppers, and onion for 10 to 12 mins, or up to they are soft.
4. Add salt, pepper, and Italian herbs for seasoning. Serve hot after giving it a good stir.

Nutrition (per serving):

Cals: 320 | Protein: 24g | Fat: 22g | Carbs: 6g | Fiber: 2g

41. HOMEMADE PORK CRACKLINGS

Prep Time: 15 mins
Cook Time: 60 mins
Total Time: 1 hr 15 mins
Servings: 6

Ingredients:

- 1 lb pork skin with fat
- 1 tbsp sea salt
- Non-compulsory: 1 tsp garlic powder or paprika (if not strict carnivore)

Instructions:

1. Turn the oven on to 300°F, or 150°C.
2. To keep the pig skin from getting soggy, scrape off any extra fat.
3. Slice the skin of the pork into tiny, bite-sized pieces.
4. Lay the skin, skin side up, on a parchment paper-lined baking sheet.
5. Season with sea salt.
6. Bake up to golden and crispy, turning halfway through, for 60 mins.
7. Before serving, let to cool.

Nutrition (per serving):

Cals: 180
Protein: 20g
Fat: 12g
Carbs: 0g

42. BEEF JERKY STRIPS

Prep Time: 10 mins
Cook Time: 4-6 hrs (dehydrator or oven)
Total Time: 4-6 hrs 10 mins
Servings: 8

Ingredients:

- 2 lbs lean beef (top round, flank, or sirloin), thinly split
- 1 tbsp salt
- Non-compulsory: 1 tsp ground black pepper or crushed red pepper

Instructions:

1. To make slicing the meat simpler, freeze it for half an hr.
2. Thinly slice the meat against the grain.
3. Add any spices and salt and toss.
4. Place the strips in a low oven (160°F/70°C) on wire racks or dehydrator trays.
5. Dehydrate up to dry yet still somewhat malleable, about 4–6 hrs.
6. Store in an airtight jar after cooling.

Nutrition (per serving):

Cals: 160
Protein: 28g
Fat: 4g, Carbs: 0g

43. CARNIVORE DEVILED EGGS

Prep Time: 15 mins
Cook Time: 10 mins
Total Time: 25 mins
Servings: 6 (12 halves)

Ingredients:

- 6 Big eggs
- 3 tbsp mayonnaise (homemade or carnivore-safe)
- 1 tsp Dijon mustard (non-compulsory)
- Salt as needed
- Cut up bacon (non-compulsory topping)

Instructions:

1. After 10 mins of boiling, let the eggs cool and peel them.
2. After halving the eggs, dump the yolks into a dish.
3. Add mayo, mustard, and salt to the yolks and mash.
4. Return Mixture to egg whites using a spoon or pipette.
5. If desired, sprinkle bacon over top.

Nutrition (per 2 halves):

Cals: 120, Protein: 6g
Fat: 10g
Carbs: 0g

44. BONE BROTH SIPPING CUPS OF

Prep Time: 5 mins
Cook Time: 12–24 hrs (simmering)
Total Time: 12–24 hrs
Servings: 8 cups of

Ingredients:

- 2 lbs beef bones (marrow or joint bones)
- 8 cups of water
- 1 tsp salt

Instructions:

1. Put the bones in a slow cooker or big saucepan.
2. Add salt and water.
3. Pressure cook for two to three hrs or simmer on low for 12 to 24 hrs.
4. After straining the broth, dispose of the solids.
5. Store in jars or pour into glasses to drink warm.

Nutrition (per cup of):

Cals: 50
Protein: 10g
Fat: 2g, Carbs: 0g

45. EGG & CHEESE CHIPS

Prep Time: 5 mins
Cook Time: 10 mins
Total Time: 15 mins
Servings: 2

Ingredients:

- 2 Big eggs
- 1/2 cup of shredded cheddar or parmesan cheese

Instructions:

1. Turn the oven on to 375°F, or 190°C.
2. Put parchment paper on a baking pan.
3. Add shredded cheese and whisked eggs.
4. Spoon Mixture in tiny circles onto baking sheet.
5. Bake up to crisp, 10 to 12 mins.
6. To get the most crunch, let cool.

Nutrition (per serving):

Cals: 170
Protein: 14g
Fat: 12g, Carbs: 1g

46. WILD BOAR ROAST

Prep Time: 20 mins

Cook Time: 2 hrs 30 mins

Total Time: 2 hrs 50 mins

Servings: 6

Ingredients:

- 3–4 lbs wild boar Muster roast
- 2 tbsp olive oil or animal fat
- 4 garlic cloves, chop-up
- 2 tsp sea salt
- 1 tsp black pepper
- 2 tsp dried rosemary
- 1 tsp thyme
- 1 onion, quartered
- 2 carrots, chop-up
- 1 cup of bone broth

Instructions:

1. Set the oven temperature to 325°F (165°C).
2. Apply olive oil, garlic, salt, pepper, rosemary, and thyme to the roast.
3. Put the carrots and onion in a roasting pan and place the roast on top.
4. Cover the roast with broth.
5. Roast for two and a half hrs, or up to soft, covered with a lid or foil.
6. Give it ten mins to rest before slicing.

Nutrition (per serving):

Cals: 450 | Protein: 48g | Fat: 26g | Carbs: 4g

47. LAMB LIVER & KIDNEY SAUTÉ

Prep Time: 10 mins

Cook Time: 15 mins

Total Time: 25 mins

Servings: 2

Ingredients:

- 6 oz lamb liver, split
- 6 oz lamb kidneys, cleaned and split
- 2 tbsp butter or tlet
- 1 garlic clove, chop-up
- 1/2 onion, split
- Salt and pepper as needed
- 1 tsp paprika (non-compulsory)

Instructions:

1. In a pan, melt the butter over medium heat.
2. Sauté the garlic and onions up to they are tender.
3. Cook the kidneys and liver for 3–4 mins on every side.
4. If using, season with paprika, salt, and pepper.
5. Serve hot, accompanied with pan juices.

Nutrition (per serving):

Cals: 340 | Protein: 35g | Fat: 21g | Carbs: 2g

48. CARNIVORE CLOUD EGGS

Prep Time: 10 mins

Cook Time: 8 mins

Total Time: 18 mins

Servings: 2

Ingredients:

- 4 eggs
- Pinch of salt
- 2 tbsp finely grated parmesan or dried beef (non-compulsory)
- Butter for greasing

Instructions:

1. Turn the oven on to 375°F, or 190°C.
2. Keep the yolks of the eggs whole while you separate the whites.
3. Add a sprinkle of salt to the whites and whip up to firm peaks form.
4. If using, fold in cheese or dry meat.
5. Line a baking sheet with parchment paper and spoon into mounds.
6. Make a well in every, then bake for three mins.
7. Top every with a yolk, then bake for another three to five mins.
8. Serve right away.

Nutrition (per serving):

Cals: 180 | Protein: 12g | Fat: 14g | Carbs: 1g

49. SCRAMBLED EGGS WITH BONE MARROW

Prep Time: 5 mins

Cook Time: 10 mins

Total Time: 15 mins

Servings: 2

Ingredients:

- 4 eggs
- 2 marrow bones, roasted and marrow scooped
- Salt as needed
- Non-compulsory: herbs like chives or parsley

Instructions:

1. Marrow bones Must be roasted for 15 to 20 mins at 450°F (230°C).
2. Over medium heat, scoop the marrow into a pan.
3. Pour the whisked eggs into the pan.
4. Gently scramble till creamy and tender.
5. If desired, add herbs and salt for seasoning. Warm up and serve.

Nutrition (per serving):

Cals: 320 | Protein: 16g | Fat: 28g | Carbs: 1g

50. BACON & EGG MUFFIN CUPS OF

Prep Time: 10 mins

Cook Time: 20 mins

Total Time: 30 mins

Servings: 6 muffins

Ingredients:

- 6 strips bacon
- 6 eggs
- Salt & pepper as needed
- Non-compulsory: shredded cheese, chives

Instructions:

1. Turn the oven on to 375°F, or 190°C.
2. Half-cook bacon in a pan up to it's not crunchy.
3. Put bacon inside muffin tin cups of.
4. Fill every cup of lined with bacon with one cracked egg.
5. Add non-compulsory cheese or herbs, salt, and pepper.
6. Bake for 15 to 20 mins, or up to eggs are set to your preference.
7. Before removing from the tin, let it cool somewhat.

Nutrition (per muffin):

Cals: 160 | Protein: 10g | Fat: 12g | Carbs: 1g

51. SOFT-BOILED EGGS IN BROTH

Prep Time: 5 mins

Cook Time: 10 mins

Total Time: 15 mins

Servings: 2

Ingredients:

- 4 Big eggs
- 3 cups of chicken or vegetable broth
- 1 tbsp soy sauce (or tamari for gluten-free)
- 1 tsp sesame oil
- 1 green onion, split
- Non-compulsory: chili oil or sesame seeds

Instructions:

1. Heat water in a saucepan up to it boils. Add the eggs gradually and cook for 6–7 mins to get soft yolks.
2. After two mins, peel the eggs and place them in cold water to stop frying.
3. Bring the broth, soy sauce, and sesame oil to a boil in a separate saucepan.
4. Place the eggs in dishes after slicing them in half.
5. Top the eggs with the hot broth and non-compulsory garnishes, such as green onions.

Nutrition (per serving):

Cals: 180 | Protein: 14g | Fat: 10g | Carbs: 4g

52. EGG YOLK CUSTARD (DAIRY-FREE)

Prep Time: 5 mins

Cook Time: 10 mins

Total Time: 15 mins

Servings: 4

Ingredients:

- 4 Big egg yolks
- 2 cups of full-fat coconut milk
- 1/4 cup of maple syrup or keto sweetener
- 1/2 tsp vanilla extract
- Pinch of salt

Instructions:

1. Whisk the egg yolks and sweetener together in a saucepan up to they are smooth.
2. Stirring continuously, gradually whisk in coconut milk and heat over medium.
3. Take off the heat as soon as it thickens (coils the back of a spoon).
4. Add a touch of salt and vanilla and stir.
5. Serve warm or chilled.

Nutrition (per serving):

Cals: 210 | Protein: 3g | Fat: 17g | Carbs: 9g

53. CREAM CHEESE OMELET ROLLS

Prep Time: 5 mins

Cook Time: 7 mins

Total Time: 12 mins

Servings: 2

Ingredients:

- 4 eggs
- 2 oz cream cheese, melted
- 1 tbsp butter or oil
- Salt and pepper as needed
- Non-compulsory: chop-up chives or smoked salmon

Instructions:

1. Beat the eggs up to they are smooth.
2. To prepare a thin omelet, heat butter on a nonstick skillet and add eggs.
3. Cook up to barely set over low heat.
4. Cover the omelet with cream cheese and top with any desired contents.
5. Serve entire or roll up and slice into pinwheels.

Nutrition (per serving):

Cals: 260 | Protein: 12g | Fat: 22g | Carbs: 2g

54. CHEESE-STUFFED MEAT LOGS

Prep Time: 10 mins

Cook Time: 25 mins

Total Time: 35 mins

Servings: 4

Ingredients:

- 1 lb ground beef or turkey
- 1/2 tsp garlic powder
- 1/2 tsp paprika
- 1/2 tsp salt
- 1/4 tsp pepper
- 4 oz mozzarella or cheddar, slice into sticks

Instructions:

1. Turn the oven on to 375°F, or 190°C.
2. Combine the ingredients with the ground beef.
3. Flatten every of the four parts, then wrap around the cheese stick.
4. Bake for 25 mins, turning halfway through, on a tray lined with paper.

Nutrition (per serving):

Cals: 310 | Protein: 27g | Fat: 22g | Carbs: 1g

55. HEAVY CREAM EGGNOG (ZERO CARB)

Prep Time: 5 mins

Cook Time: 10 mins

Total Time: 15 mins

Servings: 4

Ingredients:

- 2 cups of heavy cream
- 4 egg yolks
- 1/4 cup of erythritol or monk fruit sweetener
- 1/2 tsp nutmeg
- 1/2 tsp vanilla extract
- Non-compulsory: a splash of rum or bourbon

Instructions:

1. In a bowl, whisk the egg yolks and sweetener up to they are pale.
2. In a saucepan, heat the cream up to it's hot but not boiling.
3. Temper the yolks by slowly whisking hot milk into them.
4. Cook again up to it's thick enough to cover a spoon.
5. Add vanilla and nutmeg and stir. Serve warm or chilled with added alcohol.

Nutrition (per serving):

Cals: 340 | Protein: 3g | Fat: 35g | Carbs: 1g

56. BEEF RIBEYE STEAK WITH BONE MARROW BUTTER

Prep Time: 10 mins
Cook Time: 15 mins
Total Time: 25 mins
Servings: 2

Ingredients:

- 2 ribeye steaks (1.25–1.5 inches thick)

- Salt and pepper, as needed
- 2 bone marrow bones (split)
- 2 tbsp butter
- 1 tsp garlic powder (non-compulsory)

Instructions:

1. Set the oven temperature to 450°F (230°C). For fifteen mins, roast the bone marrow bones slice-side up.
2. In a bowl, combine the marrow, butter, and garlic powder. Put aside.
3. After patting dry, liberally season the ribeye steaks with salt and pepper.
4. A cast-iron skillet Must be heated to high heat. Sear steaks up to crusty, 2 to 3 mins per side.
5. To get the desired doneness, cook for an additional 3 to 5 mins on every side over medium heat.
6. Before serving, cover the steaks with bone marrow butter after letting them rest for five mins.

Nutrition (per serving):

Cals: 690 | Protein: 55g | Fat: 52g | Carbs: 0g

57. CRISPY CHICKEN THIGHS WITH SKIN-ON PERFECTION

Prep Time: 5 mins
Cook Time: 25 mins
Total Time: 30 mins
Servings: 4

Ingredients:

- 4 bone-in, skin-on chicken thighs
- Salt, as needed
- 1 tbsp duck fat or butter

Instructions:

1. After patting dry, sprinkle salt on the chicken thighs.
2. In a pan, heat the lard over medium heat.
3. Put the thighs skin-side down and cook them without moving for 12 to 15 mins.
4. Cook for a further 8 to 10 mins after flipping, or up to the internal temperature reveryes 165°F (74°C).

5. Give it five mins to rest before serving.

Nutrition (per serving):

Cals: 310 | Protein: 26g | Fat: 23g | Carbs: 0g

58. SAVORY BACON-WRAPPED PORK TENDERLOIN

Prep Time: 10 mins
Cook Time: 35 mins
Total Time: 45 mins
Servings: 4

Ingredients:

- 1 pork tenderloin (1–1.5 lb)
- 8–10 slices of bacon
- Salt and pepper, as needed
- 1 tsp garlic powder (non-compulsory)

Instructions:

1. Turn the oven on to 400°F, or 200°C.
2. Add salt, pepper, and garlic powder to the meat to season it.
3. Tuck the ends of the bacon pieces beneath the pig as you wrap them around it.
4. Transfer to a baking sheet or ovenproof skillet.
5. The interior temperature Must revery 145°F (63°C) after 35 to 40 mins of roasting.
6. Before slicing, let it rest for 5 to 10 mins.

Nutrition (per serving):

Cals: 420 | Protein: 35g | Fat: 30g | Carbs: 0g

59. LAMB CHOPS WITH ROSEMARY DRIPPINGS

Prep Time: 5 mins
Cook Time: 12 mins
Total Time: 17 mins
Servings: 2

Ingredients:

- 4 lamb chops

- 1 tbsp tlet or butter
- Salt, as needed
- 1 tsp dried rosemary

Instructions:

1. Use salt and rosemary to season the lamb chops.
2. In a skillet, melt the butter or tlet over medium-high heat.
3. For medium-rare, sear lamb chops for 3–4 mins on every side.
4. Before serving, let it sit in the pan juices for five mins.

Nutrition (per serving):

Cals: 480 | Protein: 38g | Fat: 36g | Carbs: 0g

60. CARNIVORE BREAKFAST SAUSAGE PATTIES

Prep Time: 10 mins
Cook Time: 10 mins
Total Time: 20 mins
Servings: 4 (8 patties)

Ingredients:

- 1 lb ground pork
- 1 tsp salt
- 1 tsp black pepper
- 1/2 tsp dried sage
- 1/2 tsp smoked paprika (non-compulsory)

Instructions:

1. In a bowl, combine the meat and spices.
2. Make eight little patties.
3. Over medium heat, heat the skillet.
4. Patties Must be cooked through and browned after 4 to 5 mins on every side.

Nutrition (per serving):

Cals: 320 | Protein: 20g | Fat: 26g | Carbs: 0g

61. GRILLED LIVER AND ONIONS (NON-COMPULSORY)

Prep Time: 10 mins
Cook Time: 10 mins
Total Time: 20 mins
Servings: 2

Ingredients:

- 1/2 lb beef liver, split
- 1 mini onion (non-compulsory for less strict carnivore)
- 1 tbsp butter or tlet
- Salt, as needed

Instructions:

1. In a pan, heat the lard over medium heat.
2. If using, add the split onions and simmer up to they are tender.
3. Set aside the onions and fry the liver slices for two to three mins on every side.
4. Serve heated, with or without onions, and season with salt.

Nutrition (per serving with onions):

Cals: 280 | Protein: 25g | Fat: 18g | Carbs: 3g
Without onions: Carbs: 0g

Made in the USA
Middletown, DE
23 May 2025